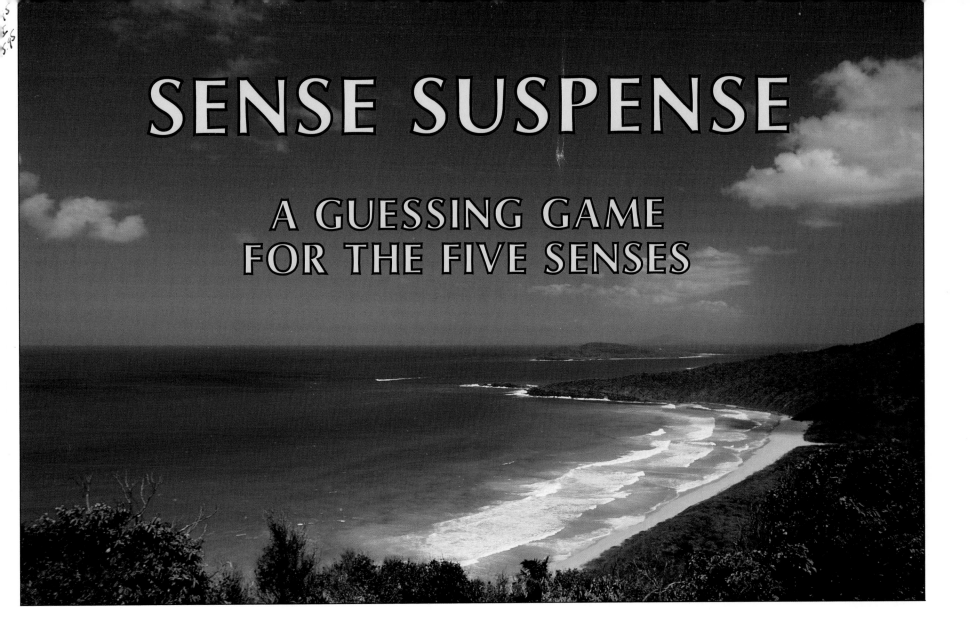

SENSE SUSPENSE

A GUESSING GAME
FOR THE FIVE SENSES

written and illustrated
with photographs and graphics by

Bruce McMillan

SCHOLASTIC
HARDCOVER

SCHOLASTIC INC. • New York

English		Español

I see  **Yo veo**
(YO VAY•o)

I touch 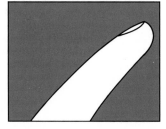 **Yo toco**
(YO TOE•co)

I smell 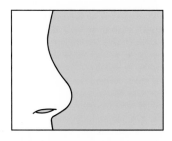 **Yo huelo**
(YO WELL•o)

I taste 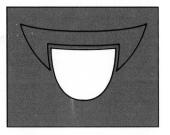 **Yo saboreo**
(YO sah•bor•RAY•o)

I hear 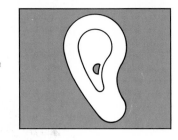 **Yo oigo**
(YO OY•go)

Which ones?

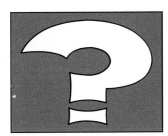

¿ Cuáles?

(KWAH • lace)

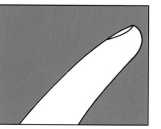
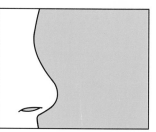
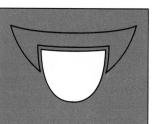
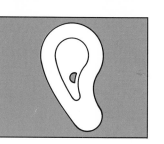

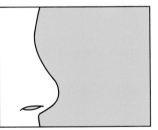
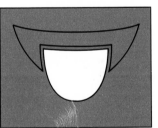
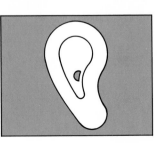

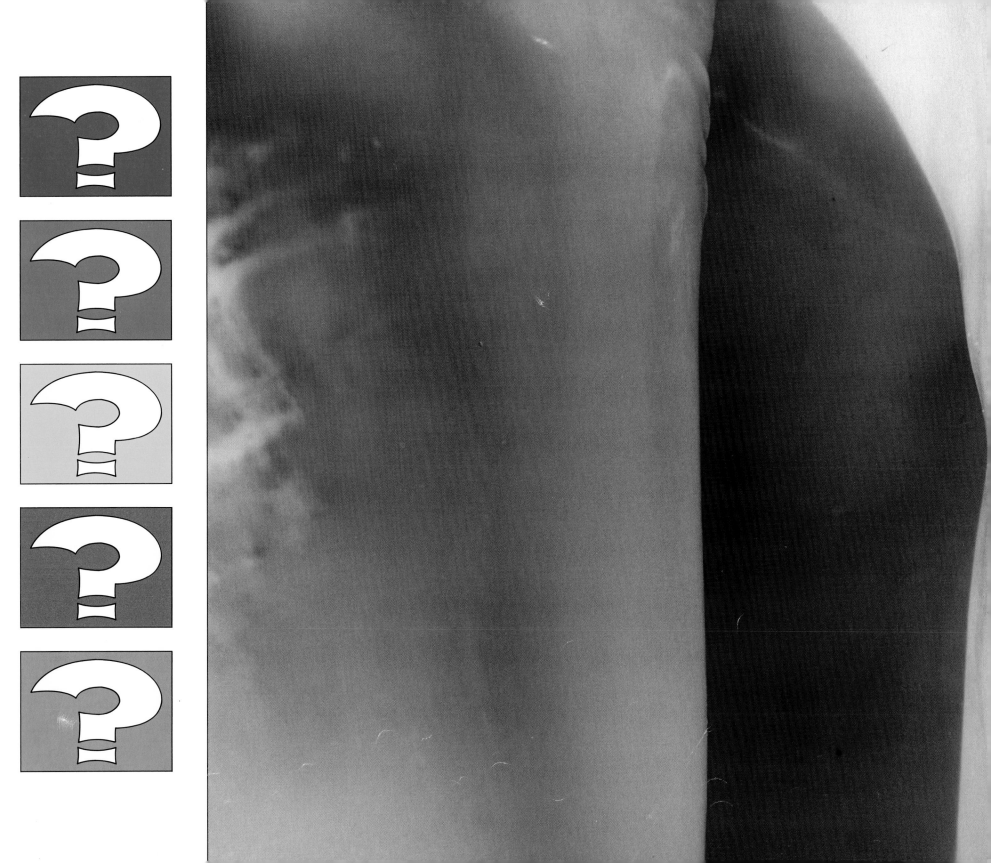

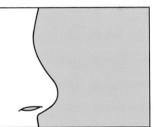
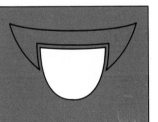
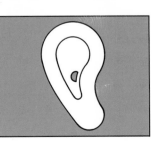

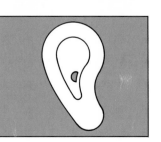

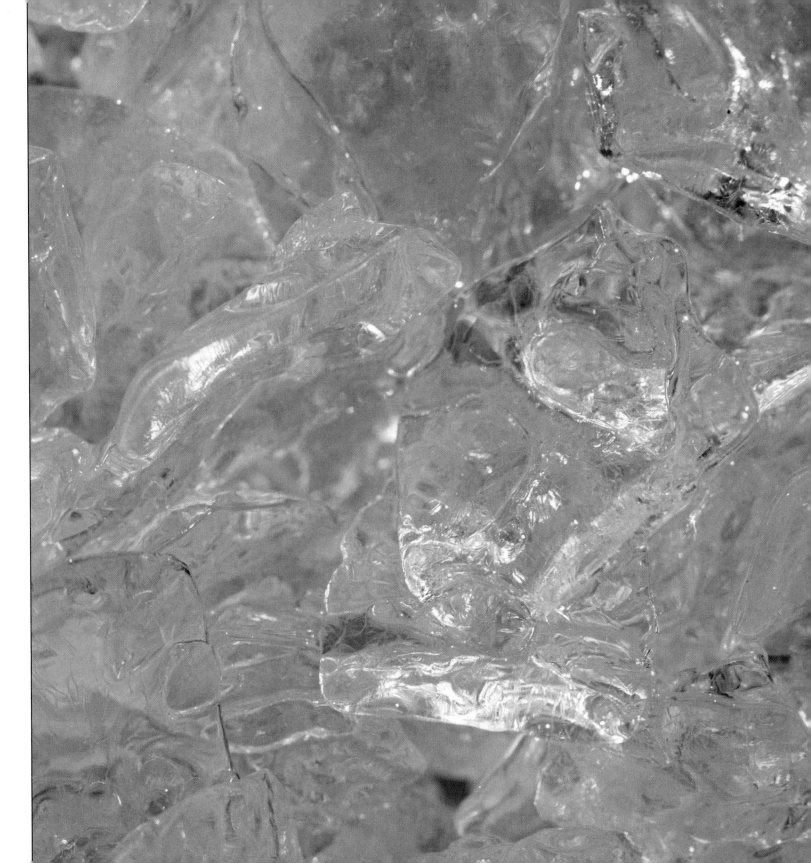

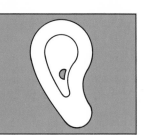

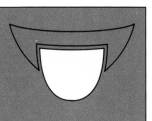

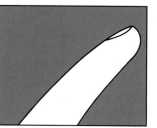

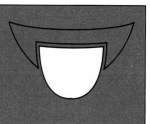
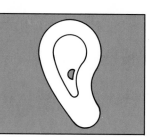

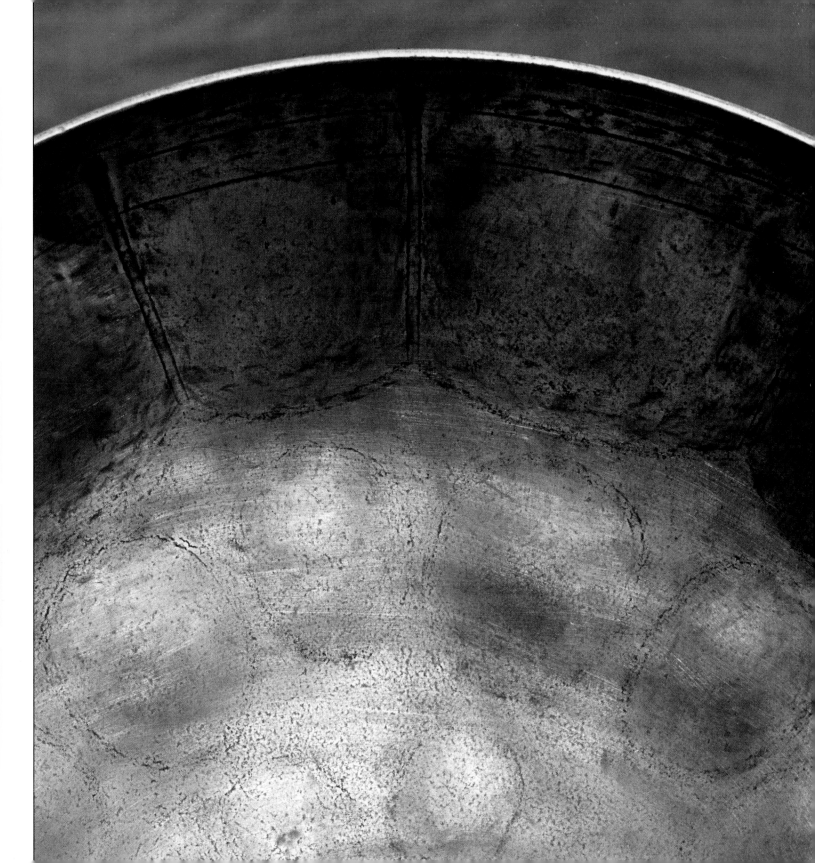

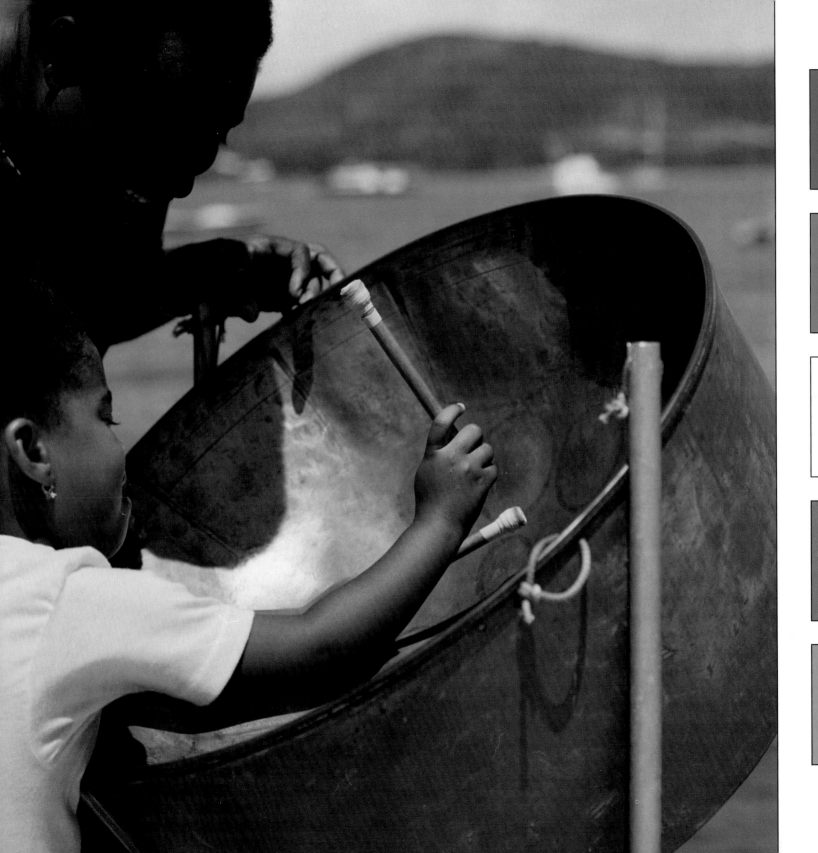

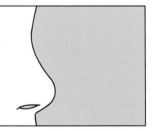

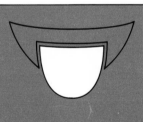
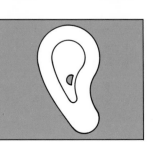

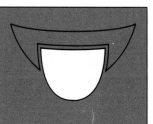
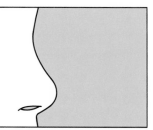
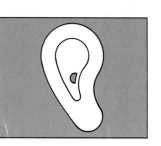

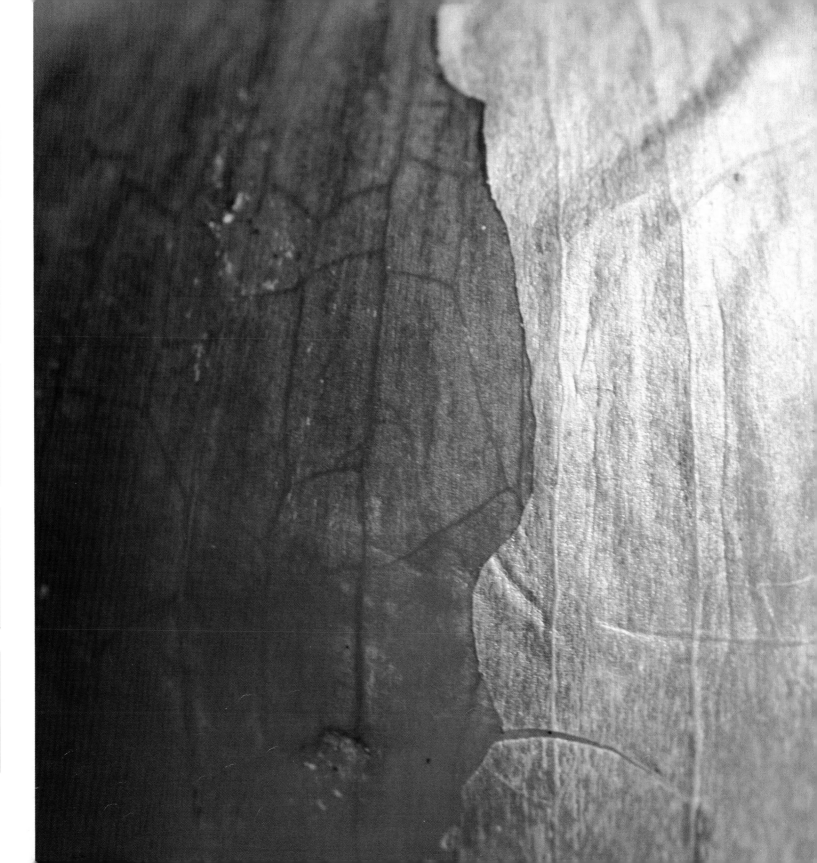

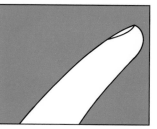
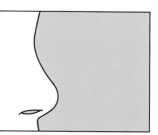
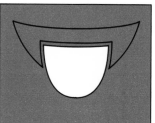
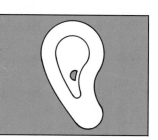

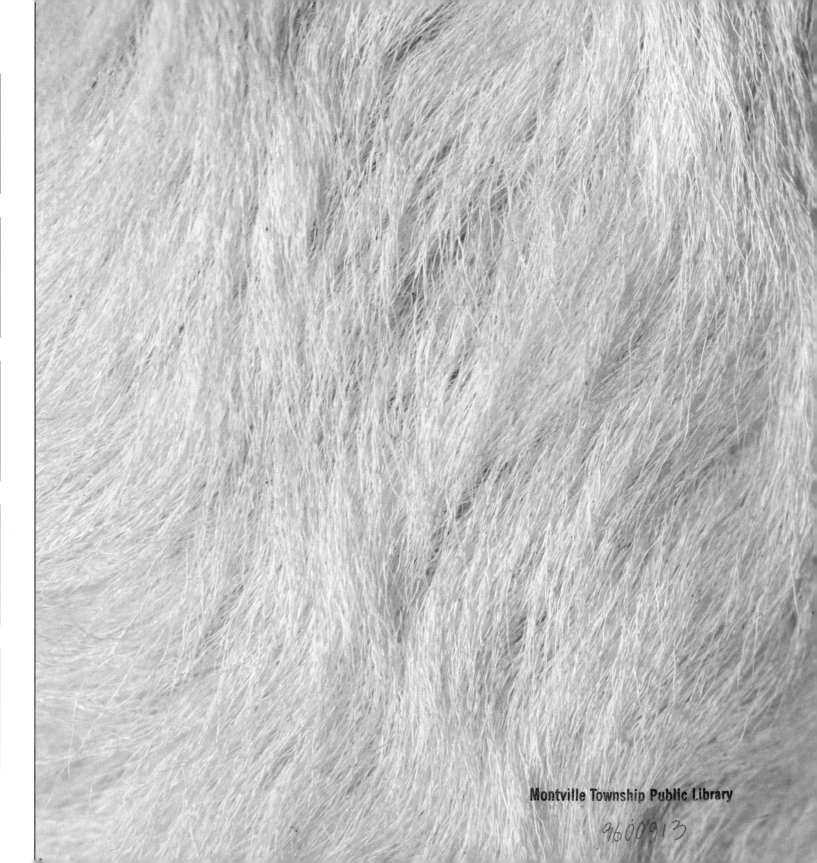

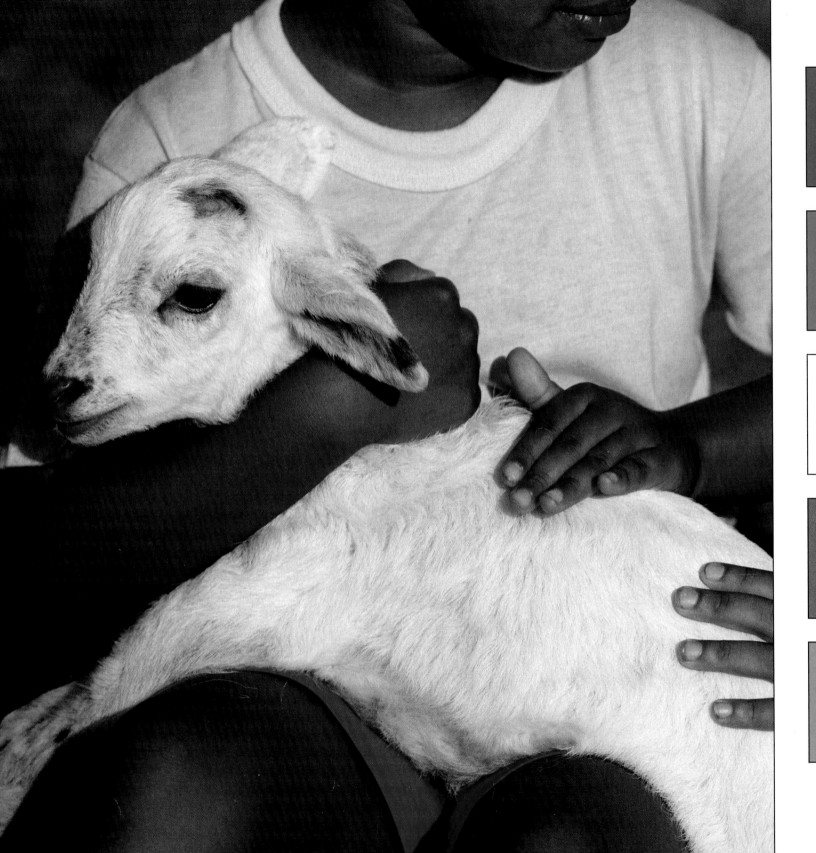

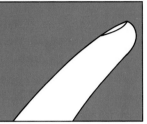
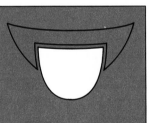
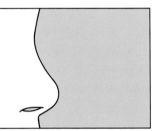

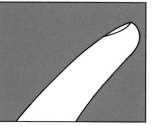
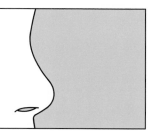
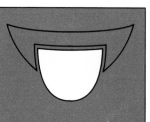
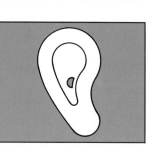

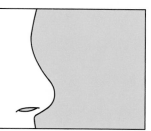
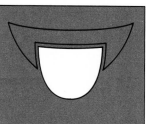
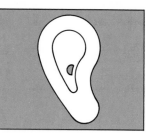

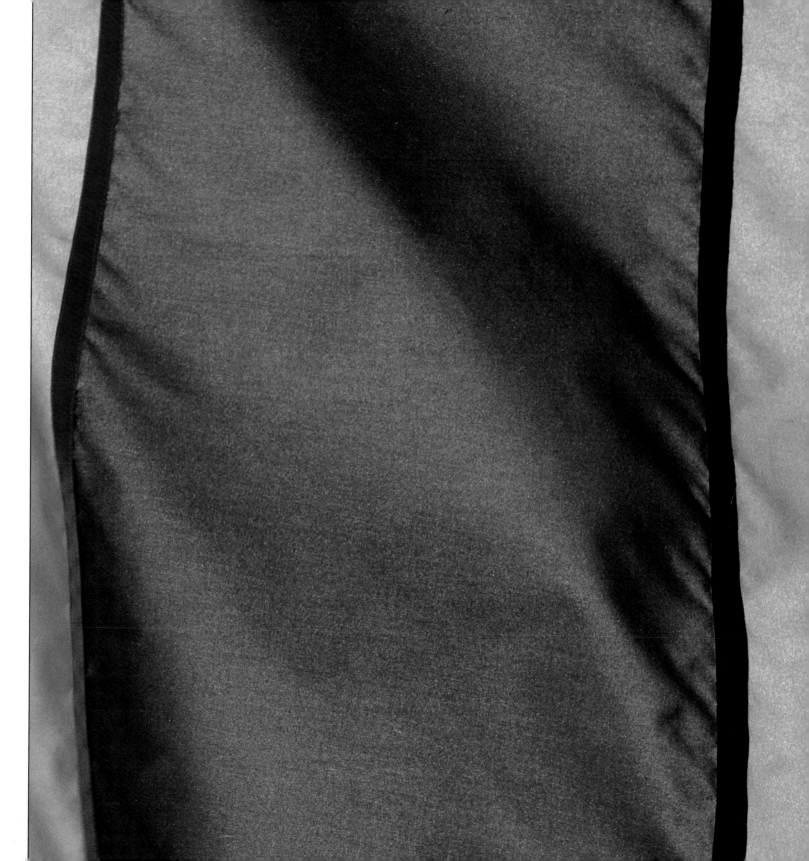

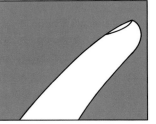
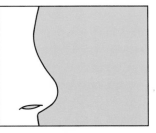
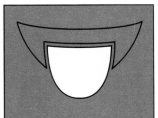
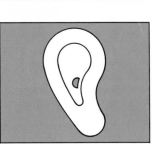

The Island of Culebra

Culebra (koo•LAY•bra), 3 miles wide (4.8 km) and 7 miles long (11.3 km), is located halfway between the Caribbean islands of Puerto Rico and St. Thomas. Once called the Spanish Virgin Island, Culebra is part of the Commonwealth of Puerto Rico.

Beverly Davis Monell and Félix García de la Cruz, the two children seen here, are among Culebra's approximately 2,000 residents. Both Spanish and English are spoken on the island, though Spanish is preferred.

White sandy beaches and coral reefs abundant with tropical fish surround the island. The climate is arid, and cactus are found throughout. Part of Culebra is a wildlife refuge and is home to over a hundred species of birds and four species of turtles, some endangered.

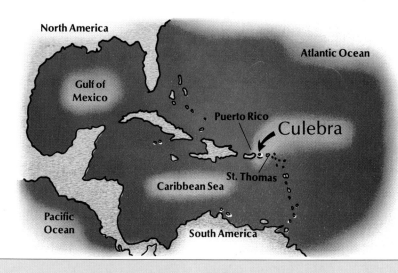

North America
Atlantic Ocean
Gulf of Mexico
Puerto Rico
Culebra
St. Thomas
Caribbean Sea
Pacific Ocean
South America

Culebra

Using this book

Since this book is a concept game, young readers will first guess what's pictured in each mysterious photo. Then, using the sense graphics, they can determine which of the five senses apply.

All of the subjects can be seen and even touched. But not all of them can be smelled, tasted, or heard. What comes to mind first? *Smelling* a flower or *seeing* it? There is no one correct answer. The following two pages offer examples of some initial sense responses. No matter what the initial response is, other senses can also be experienced. *See* it? *Touch* it? *Smell* it? *Taste* it? *Hear* it? Which ones?

So that English-speaking readers may learn some of the islanders' language, English is printed in black and the corresponding Spanish in blue. A pronunciation guide appears below each Spanish phrase.

Possible senses

taste a lollipop

see a palm tree

hear the ocean in a conch

smell a flower

touch ice

taste a drink

Algunos de los sentidos

(ahl•GOON•os DAY LOS sen•TEE•those)

saborear una paleta

(sah•bor•ray•ARE OO•nah pah•LEH•tah)

ver una palma

(VAIR OO•nah PAHL•mah)

oír en una concha el mar

(oy•YEAR EN OO•nah CONE•chah EL MAHR)

oler una flor

(o•LAIR OO•nah FLOOR)

tocar el hielo

(toe•CAHR EL YAY•lo)

saborear una bebida

(sah•bor•ray•ARE OO•nah beh•BEE•thah)

hear a steel drum  **oír un tambor de acero**
(oy•YEAR OON TAHM•bor DAY ah•SAY•ro)

touch a thorn **tocar una espina**
(toe•CAHR OO•nah es•SPEE•nah)

smell an onion **oler una cebolla**
(o•LAIR OO•nah seh•BOY•yah)

touch a kid  **tocar un cabrito**
(toe•CAHR OON cah•BREE•toe)

taste a pineapple  **saborear una piña**
(sah•bor•ray•ARE OO•nah PEEN•yah)

hear a parrot **oír un perico**
(oy•YEAR OON peh•REE•ko)

see a flag  **ver una bandera**
(VAIR OO•nah bahn•DAY•rah)

For Con

Making this book

I thank Beverly Davis Monell and Félix García de la Cruz, who were supervised by their mothers, Dominga and Carmen; Constance Compton, who worked so well with the children; and Marta Kaufman, who introduced me to Beverly and Félix. I thank the many people of Culebra who helped and participated, including steel-drumming Victor Félix Munet and flag-lowering Julio Munet Solis. Finally, I thank the talker, Sinbad the parrot.

I used a Nikon F4 with 24, 50, 55 micro, 85, 105 micro, 180, and 300mm AF Nikkor lenses, often with a polarizing filter in brilliant Caribbean daylight, with Kodachrome 64 film processed by Kodalux.

It was an especially interesting photographic experience because both the children and their mothers spoke no English, and I spoke no Spanish — at first. "¡Sonríe!" Smile. "¡Estupendo!"

Copyright © 1994 by Bruce McMillan
All rights reserved. Published by Scholastic Inc.
SCHOLASTIC HARDCOVER is a registered trademark of Scholastic Inc.
No part of this publication may be reproduced in whole or in part, or stored in a retrieval system, or transmitted in any form or by any means, electronic, mechanical, photocopying, recording, or otherwise, without written permission of the publisher.
For information regarding permission, write to
Scholastic Inc., 555 Broadway, New York, NY 10012

Library of Congress Cataloging-in-Publication Data
McMillan, Bruce
Sense suspense: a guessing game for the five senses /
written and illustrated with photographs and graphics by Bruce McMillan,   p.   cm.
ISBN 0-590-47904-0
1. Senses and sensation — Juvenile literature. [1. Senses and sensation.] I. Title.
BF233.M34   1994   152.1 — dc20   93-30272   CIP   AC
12 11 10 9 8 7 6 5 4 3 2 1   4 5 6 7 8 9/9
Printed in the U.S.A.   37   First printing, November 1994

Design by Bruce McMillan
Text set in Optima, Semi-Bold, Bold and Semi-Bold (Outline)
Color separations by Color Dot
First edition printed and bound by Berryville Graphics